The publication of this book was made possible by these sponsors

U S WEST Communications

Kawasaki Motors Manufacturing Corp., U.S.A.

Physicians Mutual Insurance Co.

Assistance in distribution was provided by

Nebraska Bankers Association

Nebraska Broadcasters Association

"Reflect on the Past,

Celebrate the Present,

Prepare for the Future"

Nebraska
THE GOOD LIFE GROWS

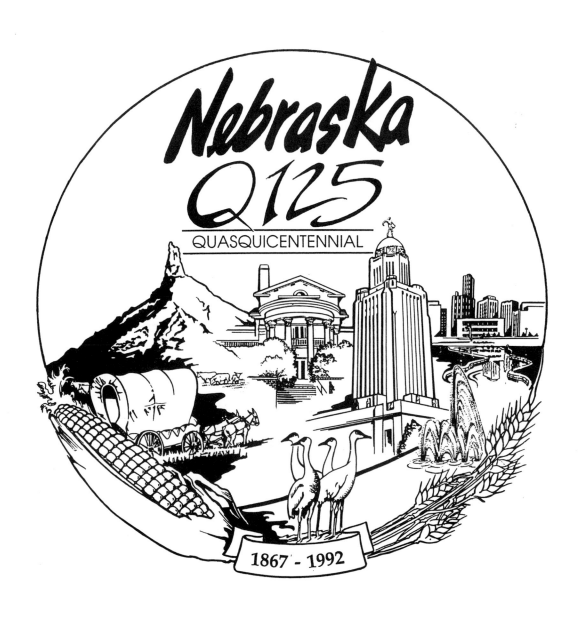

1867 - 1992

The Donning Company/Publishers
184 Business Park Drive, Suite 106
Virginia Beach, Virginia 23462

Richard A. Horwege, Editor
Eliza Midgett, Designer
Barbara A. Bolton, Project Director
Laura D. Humphrey, Project Research Coordinator
Elizabeth B. Bobbitt, Pictorial Coordinator

Library of Congress Cataloging in Publication Data:
Nebraska : the good life grows / Leonard L. Johnson, editor.
    p. cm.
    ISBN 0-89865-828-4
    1. Nebraska—Description and travel—Views.
I. Johnson, Leonard L., 1935– .
F667.054 1991   91-34270
978.2–dc20   CIP
Printed in the United States of America

Produced by the Nebraska Quasquicentennial Commission

Leonard L. Johnson, Editor

Thanks to the generous sponsors who made this volume possible:

U S WEST Communications

Kawasaki Motors Manufacturing Corp.,
U.S.A., Lincoln

Physicians Mutual Insurance Co.

Nebraska Quasquicentennial Commission:

Tri-Chairs:

Maxine Moul, Lieutenant Governor

Allen Beermann, Secretary of State

Scott Moore, State Senator, Seward

Commission Members:

Rex Amack, Lincoln

Phil Bangert, Seward

Peggy Briggs, Lincoln

Eric Brown, Lexington

Nancy Byrne, North Platte

Clay Capek, Lincoln

Lloyd Castner, Columbus

Senator Carl T. Curtis, Lincoln

Virginia Dorwart, Sidney

Steve Guenzel, Lincoln

DeMaris Johnson, Lincoln

Tom Kennedy, Newman Grove

Clark Kolterman, Seward

Hilda Kramer, Omaha

Jim Leuschen, Omaha

Jim MacAllister, Lincoln

Jane Morgan, Gordon

Clydia Nahwooksy, Lincoln

Jack Pollock, Ogallala

Lester Rhoades, Big Springs

Carol Schrader, Omaha

Marianne Simmons, Fremont

Neola Walker, Winnebago

Roger Welsch, Dannebrog

Cheryl Dahl, Q125 Celebration Coordinator

F o r e w o r d

The Otoe Indians called the place they lived *Nibrathka* which means "flat water."

Today, we call it Nebraska and it is home to nearly 1.6 million people who enjoy a culture that offers everything from champagne brunches to buffalo burgers, from ballet to powwows. Nebraska is a place where the diversity of the land—rolling grasslands, pine-covered buttes, and fertile farmlands—is mirrored in the diversity of its people.

The history of Nebraska is equally as diverse as our geography and our cultural and ethnic groups.

In the 1540s, almost 80 years before the *Mayflower* brought the Pilgrims to New England, Francisco Vasquez Coronado explored the Plains searching for gold and the fabled Quivira in a "land that is yet to be found." Although it is doubtful Coronado reached what is now Nebraska, the land had already been inhabited for thousands of years by several Indian tribes.

As Oglala Chief Red Cloud said in 1870, "Whose voice was first sounded on this land? The voice of the red people who had but bows and arrows . . . ."

Armed with little more than those bows and arrows, these original cultures flourished for centuries on the Plains, adapting to an often inhospitable climate to fashion a physical, cultural, and spiritual life in complete harmony with nature.

Nothing remains static, however, and the way of life for Indians changed forever with the coming of European explorers, traders, and missionaries. The Europeans brought with them both good and bad things that changed the culture and the lives of the Indians. They brought metal in the form of tools, weapons, and cooking utensils. They brought cloth and mirrors and blankets. Most significantly, they brought the horse that enabled tribes to cover huge distances to hunt buffalo.

The Indian people paid a high price for these luxuries. Diseases like smallpox, measles, and cholera decimated whole villages. When settlers began arriving in Nebraska in great numbers after the Civil War, they encountered not an empty wilderness but Indian tribes that were divided on whether to make peace or war as they felt their lives and livelihood being constricted.

Just as the Indian tribes—the Sioux, Omaha, Ponca, Pawnee, Otoe-Missouria, Santee—were taking a gamble on their future, new settlers to the Plains were taking a gamble on theirs.

Nebraska author Willa Cather, in the novel My Antonia, described the land, as it seemed to the first settlers, like this: "There was nothing but land; not a country at all, but the material out of which countries are made."

The newcomers to Nebraska busily started using the materials to make Nebraska. They built the railroads and planted the land to crops, they were ranchers and cowboys, they laid out towns and started schools, they raised their families and buried their dead.

The religions, the language, the food, the customs of new immigrants to Nebraska were as different as the countries from which they

Nebraska State Historical Society

Some historians say that more than half of the working cowboys in the West following the Civil War were African-Americans. One of the most famous in the 1870s was Nat Love, also known as "Deadwood Dick."

came. And they came from everywhere—from Europe, Asia, Mexico, Latin and South America, Africa, and India. Miss Cather wrote that the various settlers "spread across our bronze prairie like the daubs of color on a painter's palette."

From blue-eyed and blond-haired Nordic peoples to brown-eyed and black-skinned African-Americans, the individual contributions of the men and women who gambled on a new life in a new land joined with the contributions of Indians to shape the Nebraska of today.

Paul Olson, in the introduction to a book called *Broken Hoops and Plains People*, said conventional wisdom about immigrant groups holds that we are a melting pot in which the best of each groups' traditions fuse together to create a finer and more complete culture.

But Olson contends that the melting pot vision never did work. ". . . Every part in a coherent culture connects with every other part and with the land and sky around. A culture—an authority system, an expressive system, a way of giving and receiving gifts, of telling rights and wrong, a way of raising children and cultivating the soil—is not a TV dinner which can be packaged anywhere and used anywhere, the package unwrapped, salt and pepper added and consumed," Olson wrote. "

"Each culture worthy of the name makes some sacrifice for the greatness it achieves, and the greatness cannot be achieved without the sacrifice. Nor can one feature of the culture—even cooking—be transferred to another cultural environment unhurt any more than a good-sized cottonwood can be transplanted," Olson continued.

Dr. Susan LaFlesche Picotte, the nation's first Native American physician.

It may be true that a good-sized cottonwood probably can't be transplanted unhurt, but it is possible for the roots of strong trees to intertwine. What better time to honor our own "roots," our cultural and ethnic differences, than the 125th anniversary of Nebraska's statehood? Again this year at our annual Irish, Czech, Hispanic, Swedish, Danish, Norwegian, Polish, German, Greek, Italian, and Native American festivals we will celebrate our differences—together. Whether we swing to polkas or sway to the blues, we'll be joining hands in appreciation of each other.

This book commemorates all the people of Nebraska, whether first generation or descendants of those who crossed the Bering Strait. The pages of our history books are lined with their work, their laughter and their tears.

Following is a look at the Nebraska Hall of Fame, with inductees who have contributed immeasurably to the history of Nebraska, and then a collection of photographs contributed by professional and amateur photographers across the region that tells the story of Nebraska and its beauty.

*This photo of a powwow involving the
Santee Sioux was taken in 1918 by
P. C. Waltermire.*

Nebraska State Historical Society

The Nebraska Hall of Fame

Nebraska's past has been shaped by many. The Nebraska Hall of Fame honors those people whose talents and hard work have enriched the lives of people around the world. Whether writers or politicians, philosophers or social workers, entertainers or scientists, the eyes of these men and women saw far beyond the borders of Nebraska and life as they knew it. The horizon of their world was limited only by their imaginations and dedication . . . two qualities that the Hall of Famers had in abundance.

The Nebraska Hall of Fame was established in 1961 to officially recognize prominent Nebraskans. The Nebraska Hall of Fame Commission, with members appointed by the governor to six-year terms, is permitted to nominate one person to the Hall of Fame every two years. In 1976, the nation's bicentennial year, the commission selected four people to be honored. No person can be considered until at least 10 years after his or her death. Bronze busts of each member of the Hall of Fame are located on the second floor of the State Capitol in Lincoln. The 20 Nebraskans listed here represent the best of Nebraska and its people.

Most of the text for the Hall of Fame members was taken from the 1988–89 edition of the Nebraska Blue Book.

G*eorge* **W. Norris** (1861–1944), U.S. House of Representatives 1903–1913, U.S. Senate 1913–1943. *Initiator of reform of House rules, anti-injunction law for labor, Tennessee Valley Authority, rural electrification, Twentieth Amendment to the U.S. Constitution and sponsor of the Nebraska Unicameral Legislature. Inducted into Hall of Fame 1961.*

Willa **Cather** (1873–1947), author. *"The history of every country begins in the heart of a man or a woman" (from her book* O! Pioneers!*). In her writing about Nebraska scenes and people, Miss Cather most effectively represented the hardships, the courage, the determination and the heroic qualities of the settlers of Nebraska. Inducted into Hall of Fame 1962.*

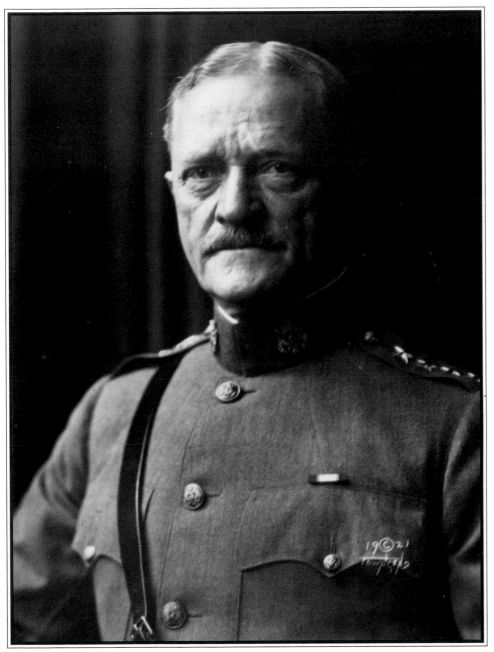

J*ohn* **J. Pershing** (1860–1949), *soldier. Commandant of cadets, University of Nebraska, 1891–1895; founder, Pershing Rifles; service, Indian Wars, Cuba, Philippines; commander, Mexican Border, 1916; commander, American Expeditionary forces, France, 1917–1919; General of the Armies of the United States, 1919; and Army chief of staff, 1921–1924. Inducted into Hall of Fame 1963–64.*

Edward J. Flanagan (1886–1948), *founder of Father Flanagan's Boys Home, Boys Town, Nebraska. "I have never found a boy who really wanted to be bad." Inducted into Hall of Fame 1965–66.*

Walter S. Graig Photography

William **Frederick Cody** (1846–1917), *a.k.a. "Buffalo Bill," soldier, buffalo hunter, Army scout, actor, rancher, irrigationist and showman of the West.* Inducted into Hall of Fame 1967–68.

William **Jennings Bryan** (1860–1925), *three-time Democratic Party nominee for president of the United States, congressman, U.S. secretary of state, orator, religious leader, and author. Inducted into Hall of Fame 1969–70.*

Bess Streeter Aldrich (1881–1954), *author. The writer, narrator of Nebraska, gave literary life to Nebraska pioneer memories and honored the trials and dreams of settlers, that all may realize and cherish their heritage.* One Aldrich novel, Λ Lantern in Her Hand, *was translated into many languages. Inducted into Hall of Fame 1971–72.*

John Gneisenau Neihardt (1881–1973), *named Nebraska Poet Laureate in 1921. Epic poet of the West, historian, philosopher and friend of the American Indian. "My God and I shall interknit as rain and ocean, breath and air; and O, the luring thought of it is prayer" (from his poem "L'Envo"). Inducted into Hall of Fame 1973–74.*

G*race Abbott* (1873–1939), *social reformer and social worker. A native Nebraskan internationally honored for her courageous and effective championship of children and mothers and for her promotion of pioneer social legislation of enduring benefit to Americans. Inducted into Hall of Fame 1975–76.*

J. Sterling Morton (1832–1902), *father of Arbor Day, U.S. secretary of agriculture, editor, farmer, legislator and Nebraska Territory secretary. "Other holidays repose upon the past, Arbor Day proposes for the future." Inducted into Hall of Fame 1975–76.*

Nathan **Roscoe Pound** (1870–1964), *botanist, pioneer ecologist, dean of University of Nebraska Law College and dean of Harvard Law School. Inducted into Hall of Fame 1975–76.*

Mari **Sandoz** (1896–1966), *novelist, historian, biographer and authority on the Plains Indians. "The real frontier lies in the stimulation of the creative mind of man." Her Great Plains series of books stands as her central achievement because of its singular interpretation of the High Plains region from the Stone Age to the twentieth century. Inducted into Hall of Fame 1975–76.*

Nebraska State Historical Society

S*tanding Bear* (1829–1908), Ponca Indian chief, symbol for Indian rights. *"I have found a better way"* (Standing Bear). *"An Indian is a person within the meaning of the law"* (landmark ruling in Standing Bear case by Judge Elmer Dundy in 1879). Inducted into Hall of Fame 1977–78.

Robert **W. Furnas** (1824–1905),
newspaperman, soldier, historian,
Nebraska governor 1873–75, and
agriculturist. He was instrumental in
creating the State Board of Agriculture
and was one of the organizers of the
Nebraska State Historical Society.
Inducted into Hall of Fame 1979–80.

Nebraska State Historical Society

Edward Creighton (1820–1874), telegraph pioneer and banker. He cherished a desire to establish a college where young men might enjoy the educational advantages denied him. Funds from his estate and contributions from his brother, John Andrew Creighton, helped found Creighton University in 1878. Inducted into Hall of Fame 1981–82.

Susette LaFlesche Tibbles

(1854–1903), Omaha Indian, a.k.a.
"Inshata Theumba" or "Bright Eyes,"
speaker and writer for Indian rights.
Inducted into Hall of Fame 1983–84.

Nebraska State Historical Society

Nebraska State Historical Society

Gilbert **M. Hitchcock** (1859–1934), *newspaperman and politician. Founder of the* Omaha World-Herald *in 1889; U.S. House of Representatives 1902–1904 and 1906–1911; U.S. Senate 1911–1922. Inducted into Hall of Fame 1985–86.*

Loren **Eiseley** (1907–1977), anthropologist, poet and philosopher of science. "His clear expositions constitute a brilliant history of man's scientific thought about the world in which he lives." Eiseley was awarded 36 honorary degrees and was a visiting professor at many universities, including Harvard, Columbia, Stanford and Yale. Inducted into Hall of Fame 1987–88.

Nebraska Hall of Fame

Hartley **Burr Alexander** (1873– 1939), *anthropologist, poet, philosopher, educator and authority on North American Indian mythology. Best known as author of the symbolism and inscriptions on the Nebraska State Capitol and other buildings across the United States. Inducted into Hall of Fame 1989–90.*

Arthur Weimar Thompson

(1886–1970), *premier auctioneer. In a 46-year career, Thompson called more than 7,500 livestock sales from New York to California and from Canada to Mexico. World's Who's Who recognized Thompson as "the leading purebred livestock auctioneer in the United States and Canada." Inducted into Hall of Fame 1991–92.*

"Reflect on the Past,

Celebrate the Present,

Prepare for the Future"

Chimney Rock south of Bayard in the Nebraska Panhandle was the most-mentioned natural landmark recorded in diaries of those heading west in covered wagons on the Oregon Trail in the 1800s. It served as a milestone to gauge distance traveled and has become a symbol of Nebraska.

Oregon Trail Museum Association

Some of the ruts made by the wheels of covered wagons pulled by horses and oxen are still visible on parts of the Oregon and Mormon trails in the Nebraska Panhandle.

Omaha Chamber of Commerce

The Mormon Pioneer Cemetery in north Omaha is the burial site for nearly 600 Mormons who died of disease and exposure during the winter of 1846–47 as they camped at the site waiting for spring to resume their trek west.

David Hendee, Omaha

The Sand Hills of north-central Nebraska are among the wonders of the world, covering more than 19,300 square miles in all or parts of 23 counties. This photo, taken along Nebraska Highway 2, shows the natural beauty of the Sand Hills.

(Photo right) There have been many theories advanced on the origin of the custom started in the 1940s of placing worn-out cowboy boots on fence posts. Some say they denote the number of sons in the ranch family, or the number of high school graduates in the family, while others say the toes point to the main house in case a traveler is lost in a storm. One of the most likely explanations is that "cowboys live here."

Nebraska Department of Economic Development

Jail Rock and Courthouse Rock are among the many intriguing formations bordering the North Platte River Valley along the Oregon Trail in the Panhandle near Bridgeport. They also served as early-day mileposts.

This fairy ring of lovegrass, which may be centuries old, can be seen on a hillside along Nebraska Highway 27 in Old Jules Country near Gordon.

Kira Gale, Omaha

The names of some of the natural landmarks in Nebraska sometimes are as interesting as the landmarks themselves. This photo (left) shows Pair of Pants Butte in the Pine Ridge's Sowbelly Canyon near Harrison.

Little can surpass the beauty of a June morning in the Samuel R. McKelvie National Forest southwest of Valentine in the S...

Sheridan's Gates north of Camp Sheridan, an old military post in Sheridan County northeast of Chadron, demonstrates the beauty of the area. The land now is private property.

A stone house was a rarity on the plains of Nebraska, but it stood the weather better than wooden structures. This abandoned structure is west of Stockville in Frontier County.

Mary and Nancy Schaffert, Curtis

With the first frost of autumn comes the morning mist in the Old Jules orchard valley.

Bison are raised in the Pine Ridge at Fort Robinson State Park. They supply meat for the famed buffalo stew served at many of the Game and Parks Commission state parks across Nebraska.

Toadstool Park, located in the Oglala National Grasslands in extreme northwest Nebraska, offers the beauty of rock formations found nowhere else in the state.

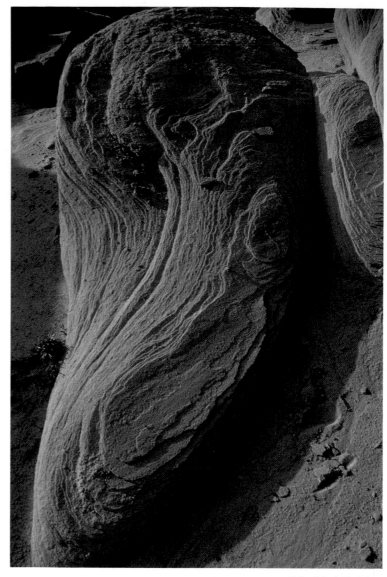

Nature's windblown artistry can sometimes create eerie images in the visitor's mind at Toadstool Park.

An early morning scene looking west in the old Niobrara State Park near Niobrara in Knox County. When the park was moved to the top of nearby hills because of flooding from the backwaters of Lewis and Clark Lake, the old park was allowed to return to its natural environment with minimal maintenance.

Mark Dietz, Bellevue

A bull elk takes a good look at the photographer at the Fort Niobrara National Wildlife Refuge near Valentine.

Jim Taylor, Stuart

A little-known scene that grabs the eye is Rock Falls in Holt County. The falls are on Eagle Creek about 16 miles northeast of Atkinson on private land owned by Albert Widtfeldt.

Fall is a beautiful time of the year, but nowhere is it more beautiful than at Ponca State Park, just north of Ponca in northeast Nebraska's Dixon County. Ponca is one of seven state parks in Nebraska.

"Framed" is the title of this photo showing some of the old fort at Fort Hartsuff State Historical Park near Burwell. An active post from 1874 to 1881, all the major buildings at Fort Hartsuff have been reconstructed for interpretive purposes.

Fresh snow helps set off the barn at Buffalo Bill's Ranch State Historical Park at North Platte. There are 10 state historical parks in Nebraska.

The log cabin of Daniel Freeman, the first man to file a claim under the Homestead Act, is one of the attractions of Homestead National Monument near Beatrice in Gage County.

Kent Klima, Omaha

The girlhood home of famed Nebraska author Willa Cather is among the many landmarks in and around Red Cloud in Webster County that tell visitors they are in Catherland.

Dawn of a misty fall day at Indian Cave State Park in southeast Nebraska's Nemaha and Richardson counties can offer a spectacle of beauty.

People in period costumes are part of the living history events that mark Catherland.

A *tepee that can be rented by campers is one of the many offerings of Platte River State Park west of Louisville in Cass County.*

Attesting to the raw beauty of the Platte River valley in the fall is this shot taken looking east from Platte River State Park.

Janet McKenzie, Omaha

Living history is part of the excitement offered by Fort Atkinson State Historical Park near Fort Calhoun in Washington County.

A true Nebraska landmark is Arbor Lodge, the restored mansion of J. Sterling Morton, founder of Arbor Day. The lodge is located in Arbor Lodge State Historical Park at Nebraska City in Otoe County.

The National Arbor Day Foundation is developing a unique educational complex on what was once the agricultural estate of J. Sterling Morton in Nebraska City. Part of the complex is the Apple House. The National Arbor Day Center will be the only educational facility of its kind in the nation, with programs and staff dedicated to tree planting, conservation and environmental stewardship. The foundation has provided millions of trees to tree planters across the nation.

"Reflect on the Past,

Celebrate the Present,

Prepare for the Future"

Jim Denney, Omaha

Eugene T. Mahoney State Park, which opened in May 1991, is the crown jewel of the Nebraska Game and Parks Commission's park system. The 574-acre layout is the only one of the state parks designed for year-round use. Shown is the Peter Kiewit Lodge and Restaurant, which offers forty rooms. Besides the lodge, there are forty cabins and hookups for 149 RV's, plus tent camping.

Among the amenities at Eugene T. Mahoney State Park near Ashland, between Omaha and Lincoln, is the heated Richard L. Coyne Pool with two diving boards and a 236-foot water slide. There also is a riding stable, a golf driving range, miniature golf, a marina, a conservatory, tennis courts, an observation tower, a fishing lake, a theater, hiking trails and crafts center.

Jim Denney, Omaha

The Nebraska State Fair, held each year in Lincoln, is one of the biggest attractions in the state. Besides the midway carnival rides, the fair hosts the state's largest livestock show and offers judging in everything from fruits and vegetables to sewing and baking.

Janet McKenzie, Omaha

On July 3, 1991, Omaha celebrated the return of troops from Operation Desert Storm with a parade honoring veterans of all wars and a free show featuring singer John Denver and Chip Davis of Mannheim Steamroller in Rosenblatt Stadium. The Desert Storm troops served in the Middle East with the United Nations troops that forced Iraq to withdraw from Kuwait.

Thousands of spectators lined the parade route along South Thirteenth Street as Omaha honored the veterans of all wars. More than 20,000 people packed Rosenblatt Stadium for the free show and fireworks display that followed.

Wilber, officially designated as the Czech Capital of the USA, held its 30th annual Czech Festival in 1991. Among the many events at the three-day festival is the crowning of Miss Czech USA. Shown are a group of state Czech queens competing in the national contest in 1990.

Todd R. Leif, Concordia, Kansas

The melon feed is just one of the many events that get the spotlight during Turkey Days at Oxford, proclaimed the Turkey Capital of Nebraska.

The powwow held each August in Macy is one of the celebration highlights of the year for the Omaha Indians. It attracts hundreds of people from throughout the Midlands each year.

Stephen Provost

The Sandhillbillies, a musical group from Stuart, perform at events throughout the area. Shown is Rollie Kung, a member of the group.

Jim Taylor, Stuart

Gladys Phillips, Beaver Crossing

Old Glory hangs from a streetlight as opposing teams of firefighters battle with hoses to control the red, white and blue barrel during the water fight event at Seward's annual July 4 celebration. Seward lays claim to having the biggest Fourth of July festival in the state.

Flags wave proudly in the forefront as the honor guard leads the parade at the Beemer Centennial.

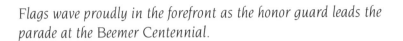

The official Nebraska Balloon is owned and operated by Gary and Judy Cass of Plattsmouth. It served as the logo for the Celebrate Nebraska events around the state in 1988. Cass contracts with various festivals to fly the balloon during their celebrations. It has flown in balloon events in twenty-five states, plus Mexico and Japan.

Colorful dancers were among the stage high-lights of the fourth annual Hispanic Heritage Festival held in Lincoln in September 1990.

Nobody has more fun than the kids at the Box Butte County Fair. The fair is held each August in Hemingford.

Todd R. Leif, Concordia, Kansas

A patriotic reflection in the steel helmet of a
member of the honor guard provided the
opportunity for an unusual photograph. The
event was a Memorial Day service at Hastings.

Harry Younglund, Stromsburg

The annual Swedish Festival at Stromsburg attracts hundreds of visitors each year to watch the parade, enjoy stage shows, and sample its famous smorgasbord.

The annual Fourth of July fireworks display at Rosenblatt Stadium, initiated by the Omaha World-Herald, has become a tradition. Thousands of people pack the ball park and park for miles around to witness the display. This photo was taken from Fontenelle Forest.

Mark Dietz, Bellevue

An American Legion honor guard presents the colors at the Cheney Cemetery southeast of Lincoln on Memorial Day.

James L. Fly, Lincoln

When the Mad Dads of Omaha organized to help lead youths away from street gangs, they received national attention. Here, President George Bush honored the organization when he spoke in Omaha in June 1990.

Orville Jones III, Lincoln

Earth Day, April 22, is rapidly gaining a foothold in the fabric of American culture. Here, a design is constructed out of recyclable products by a participant at Memorial Park in Omaha in 1990.

Janet McKenzie, Omaha

One of the most festive events in central Nebraska is the annual lighting of the Kearney County Courthouse Christmas lights in Minden. Thousands of lights are used in the display. The community also puts on a Christmas program on the courthouse grounds several times each yuletide season.

Jim Denney, Omaha

One of the most colorful festivals of the year is staged each St. Patrick's Day at O'Neill. Painting a large clover leaf on the intersection in the downtown area is just one of the ways the organizers say "We're Irish."

Jim Denney, Omaha

Omaha's River City Roundup, staged in September each year to coincide with the Ak-Sar-Ben Rodeo and Livestock Show, is one of the state's biggest festivals. Preliminary promotions include a Trail Ride starting at Ogallala and a steam engine group tour that starts at North Platte. One of the many events in Omaha include a televised downtown parade, featuring giant balloons. Shown here is the Buster the Crab balloon.

River City Roundup

Leonard Holling, Omaha

On July 30, 1988, a group of 328 volunteers converged on the Herman Ostry farm just outside Bruno in Butler County to help Ostry move his nine-ton, two-story barn. The participants, using specially built lifting bars, picked up the barn with their hands and moved it 143 feet 8 inches to a new location. In July 1989, another group of volunteers lifted the barn about 10 inches onto its foundation.

Using special lifting bars anchored inside and outside the Ostry barn, the volunteers moved it.

David City Banner-Press

Bill Bieck, McCook

The beauty of Heritage Hills Golf Course in McCook is apparent as the photographer shot across the front nine holes on the links course during the early morning. The course was named one of the nation's 75 best public golf courses in 1984 by Golf Digest.

There are trees aplenty to play havoc with errant shots at Elmwood Park Golf Course in Omaha.

Janet McKenzie, Omaha

77

Janet McKenzie, Omaha

An exercise boy takes a Thoroughbred for an early morning workout at Ak-Sar-Ben in Omaha. Pari-mutuel racing at Ak-Sar-Ben is one of the biggest attractions for out-of-state visitors and Nebraskans alike.

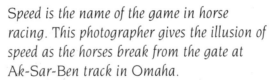

Kate McGuire, Wood River

Speed is the name of the game in horse racing. This photographer gives the illusion of speed as the horses break from the gate at Ak-Sar-Ben track in Omaha.

No, it is not too flat to ski in Nebraska. NebraSKI is located just off Highway 6 between Lincoln and Omaha. Sometimes, artificial snow is added to the real thing to keep the slopes in shape for skiers.

Nebraska Department of Economic Development

Todd R. Leif, Concordia, Kansas

One of the most dedicated of all athletes is the triathlete, who must endure rigorous training to compete in the triathlon, a competition of bicycling, swimming, and running. Here, the photographer captured a triathlete training on the bike near Hastings as he rides into the sunset.

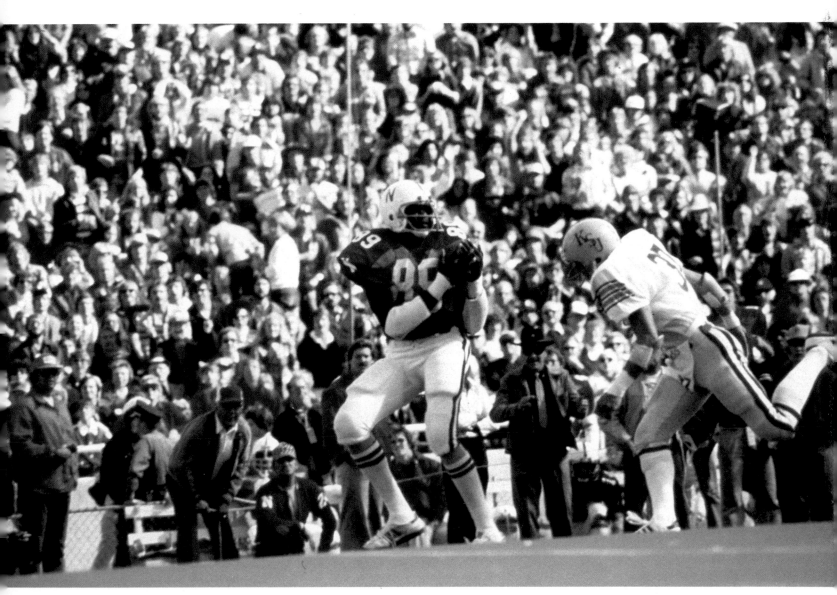

Performing in front of a sea of 76,000 red-clad football fans is one of the fondest memories of Nebraska Cornhusker players who have suited up at Memorial Stadium in Lincoln. The stadium becomes the states' third-largest city on football Saturdays.

The biggest athletic event of the year in Nebraska is the Cornhusker State Games, where more than 15,000 participants compete in 29 major sport categories. The games, started in Lincoln in 1985, have grown each year and soccer has become the sport with the greatest number of entries.

Cornhusker State Games

The Road Race is one of the features of the Cornhusker State Games, which attracts participants from nearly every county in Nebraska. The sports festival is held the third weekend in July in and around Lincoln.

Cornhusker State Games

Richard Hamilton, Stuart

Things don't get much more tranquil than fishing from the bank for walleyes at sunset at Merritt Reservoir in the Sand Hills southwest of Valentine.

Richard Hamilton, Stuart

It is never too early to get the fishing bug. Here, Janeen Hamilton shows off a "lunker" taken from a farm pond while ice fishing in the Sand Hills.

Omaha's Rosenblatt Stadium is the site of the NCAA College World Series in June each year, as well as the home of the Omaha Royals AAA baseball team.

Recreation draws community support in many towns. And nothing captures the beauty of small-town enjoyment better than this shot of a Friday night slow-pitch softball game in Louisville.

Burwell hosts "Nebraska's Big Rodeo" in July each year, and the entertainment doesn't stop with the rodeo events at the fairgrounds arena. Besides wild horse and chuckwagon races, there is a carnival, art and quilt shows, and the Miss Rodeo Nebraska Pageant.

Jim Denney, Omaha

For those who love the adventure of canoeing, the Niobrara River east of Valentine is one of the state's premiere locations. Here, Larry Novicki and his son, Mark, from Omaha, negotiate Fritz's Rapids southeast of Sparks.

John Melingagio, Omaha

Nebraska is known for its sunsets and its many churches. Combine the two and you have a sight to behold.

Trinity Lutheran Church near Murdock is a classic rural church as it dominates the countryside.

The beauty of a stained-glass window is inspiring at the Father Flanagan tomb in Dowd Memorial Chapel at Boys Town.

The Episcopal Church at Santee on Lewis and Clark Lake offers
a spirit of reverence to the beauty of the surroundings.

Jim Denney, Omaha

St. Cecelia's Cathedral has been a central Omaha landmark for years. For those who have seen only the giant twin spires outside, this photo offers a view of the magnificent interior.

The Tower of the Four Winds, a monument to Black Elk, an Oglala Sioux holy man, is located in Black Elk-Neihardt Park in Blair, adjacent to the Dana College campus. The tower, designed by the late F. W. "Bill" Thomsen of Blair, was dedicated in 1987. The 44-foot-tall monument is faced with glass mosaic and was financed by private donations and grants raised by a non-profit corporation. A city water reservoir forms a backdrop for the monument.

Les Hosick, Stockville

Jim Denney, Omaha

The French Chapel has a beauty all its own on the Hastings College campus.

Dancing Leaf Earth Lodge is located on the banks of Medicine Creek just north of Stockville in Frontier County. The 20 x 20-foot igloo-shaped structure is a replica of those found in the area that archaeologists identify as belonging to the Upper Republican Culture, farming people who were probably ancestors of the Pawnee Indians.

The Watson Ranch, 26 miles north of Scottsbluff on State Highway 71, offers an unusual sight to passers-by. Although windmills are common in Nebraska's farming regions, this cluster of seven windmills earns a second glance from many, and an unusual photo opportunity when the sun is setting.

Kent Klima, Omaha

Migrant farm workers are an important part of the agricultural economy in some areas of Nebraska. Shown here are migrant workers weeding a sugar beet field in the Scottsbluff area.

Nebraska Association of Farmworkers

Before center-pivots became popular in recent years, most irrigation was done by canal ditches with tubes, or as shown here, by irrigation pumps with gated pipe releasing water in the corn rows.

Robin Phillips, Beaver Crossing

The large number of irrigated acres in Nebraska has helped many farmers tough out the recent drought years. From the air, this photo almost turns the circular green fields of corn against the backdrop of yellow wheat fields into an art project. The aerial photo of center-pivot irrigation systems was taken north of Friend.

Gladys Phillips, Beaver Crossing

Nebraska Department of Economic Development

And this is what it looks like from ground level as the giant center-pivot irrigation systems cover more than 150 acres each.

Jim Denney, Omaha

Being able to plow a straight furrow has always been one measure of the ability of a farmer. This farmer five miles north of Hartington in Cedar County wouldn't take a back tractor seat to anyone.

Gladys Phillips, Beaver Crossing

At the Monahan Cattle Company's Circle Dot ranch northeast of Hyannis in Grant County, young cowboys are shown on a hillside above Collins Lake, which was drained to provide meadows from which to harvest hay.

Modern farming has passed by this old implement, but it still poses a beautiful sight against the setting sun.

Jim Denney, Omaha

Hay stacks have taken on a different look in Nebraska in recent years with the advent of large circular "bales."

From late June through July, the drone of combines harvesting the winter wheat crop can be heard in the countryside. Dryland wheat is the lifeblood of thousands of farmers in western Nebraska, where irrigation for other cash crops often is not feasible.

Clarke S. Nelson, Holdrege

"Grain in the Bin" is the title of this photo taken of a truck delivering its load at a grain elevator.

Jim Denney, Omaha

Nebraska is known for its "skyscrapers" of the plains. This grain elevator east of Hastings is one of the most imposing structures.

When the elevators fill up and there are not enough rail cars to move the grain, it is sometimes piled on the ground. This pile of milo was at the Blue Valley Coop at Tamora.

Every once in a while, nature can use a helping hand. Here, Maynard Schulze of Tilden bottle feeds an orphaned calf.

Ranch life is not all work and no play. Shown here are some ranch hands at a Sunday afternoon calf-roping get-together at Alliance.

Rounding up strays can stretch a cowboy's day into the sunset hours. This shot was taken in the Sand Hills near Thedford in Thomas County.

Nebraska Game and Parks Commission

Cattle drives aren't what they used to be, but they still are a fact of life in Nebraska's ranch country. Here, a cowboy gets help from a pickup as they drive cattle on a ranch northeast of Harrison in Sioux County.

One important chore in life on a ranch is the branding that must be done after the spring calf crop. This branding operation photo was taken on the West Spear Ranch south of Nenzel in Cherry County.

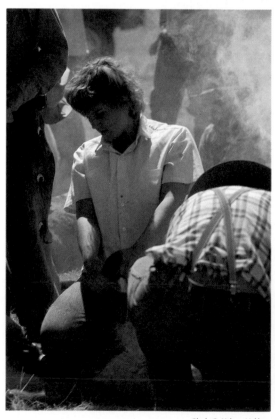

Clarke S. Nelson, Holdrege

The holding pens at the Omaha Stockyards used to be the busiest in the nation, but the dispersal of packing plants to rural towns closer to the livestock production has caused Omaha to lose its title as the meat-packing center of the United States.

Janet McKenzie, Omaha

Oil exploration was a booming business in Nebraska 30 years ago, with major fields discovered in southwest Nebraska and the Panhandle. Oil is still being pumped from hundreds of wells, such as this one near Gurley in Cheyenne County, but exploration and production have seen better days.

Jim Denney, Omaha

One industry that can be seen for miles around is the Ash Grove cement plant at Louisville in Cass County. The plant was built in 1929 and has a capacity of 1 million tons of cement a year. The company has been shipping about 750,000 tons a year to contractors throughout the Midwest.

Jim Denney, Omaha

Fred Veleba, Omaha World-Herald

The year 1975 was a big one for weather calamities in eastern Nebraska. In January, a blizzard dumped between 11 and 16 inches of snow and virtually shut down the Omaha metropolitan area. Here, a motorist tries to negotiate a road in the Blue Ridge Addition in Sarpy County after it was plowed open.

S. J. *Melingagio*, Omaha World-Herald

More devastating than the blizzard a few months earlier was the killer tornado that ripped through Omaha in May 1975. Miraculously, only three people lost their lives as the tornado carved out a swath from southwest Omaha to the central part of the city. This photo was taken in the Westgate area shortly after the storm passed. Officials estimated the total amount of damage from the tornado at $112.45 million.

A lone tree stands vigil in a Sand Hills ground blizzard that saw the windchill index reach 60 below zero.

Richard Hamilton, Stuart

107

Nebraska's sometimes harsh weather can offer a glimmer of beauty, as in this photo of an approaching thunderstorm taken in Cheyenne County.

David Hendee, Omaha

Jim Denney, Omaha

Lake McConaughy plays host to a number of events throughout the summer, but one of the biggest is the annual Labor Day Governor's Cup Regatta.

Landlocked Nebraska doesn't suffer in comparison with other states when it comes to water. Natural and man-made lakes offer the pleasures of water sports, besides providing flood control and irrigation. Nebaska's largest lake is Lake McConaughy, north of Ogallala in Keith and Garden counties. Big Mac, with 35,000 surface acres and 105 miles of natural sandy beach shoreline, attracts nearly 700,000 people annually and is one of Nebraska's top attractions for out-of-state visitors.

Jack Pollock, Ogallala

Smith Falls, (left) the highest falls in the state at more than 70 feet, is located on private land on Smith Creek, about a quarter-mile south of the Niobrara River south of Sparks in Cherry County.

Mary and Nancy Schaffert, Curtis

Johnson Lake, southwest of Lexington in Gosper County, is a man-made beauty, even when it is ice-locked in mid-winter.

Jim Denney, Omaha

Enders Reservoir in Chase County is a U.S. Bureau of Reclamation impoundment that provides flood control and irrigation besides a multitude of recreational opportunities.

Lake Hayes at Camp Duke Alexis in Hayes County offers a peaceful respite for southwest Nebraskans.

Mary and Nancy Schaffert, Curtis

The North Loup River valley is a natural
beauty in the fall as the river winds its way
near Scotia in Greeley County.

Lake Hastings offers tranquility and beauty,
especially as it captures the dimming rays of
the setting sun in the Queen City.

Lake Maloney south of North Platte in Lincoln County has been a popular fishing lake in Nebraska for many years.

117

Rocky Ford Rapids on the Niobrara River southeast of Sparks offers a bit of a test for those in canoes, so they are advised to portage, but otherwise the rapids just add beauty to the magnificent scenery.

Jim Denney, Omaha

The Frank House in Kearney, whose exterior has been restored to its original state when it was built by banker-investor George Washington Frank in 1889, is on the campus of the University of Nebraska at Kearney. From 1904 to 1911, it served as the state's first tuberculosis hospital. The state deeded the property to Kearney State College in 1972 and the university now maintains the property.

Jim Denney, Omaha

Janet McKenzie, Omaha

The first music from the Henningson Memorial Campanile on the University of Nebraska at Omaha campus was heard in November 1988. The 168-foot carillon has 47 bells.

Skinner Mall on the campus of Creighton University in Omaha is a place for students to meet and study when the weather cooperates. This scene shows the historic St. John's Church and the Administration Building in the background.

120

The campus of Doane College in Crete, with swans on Doane Lake, is one of the most beautiful in the state. The college, established in 1872, is one of the oldest private colleges in Nebraska.

Jim Denney, Omaha

The main stage theater of the Lied Center for Performing Arts seats 2,210 people and is one of three stages in the center. The nonparallel walls and custom seating in the hall were designed to create perfect acoustics.

Tom Tidball, University of Nebraska, Lincoln

The most imposing building on the University of Nebraska, Lincoln campus is the Lied Center for Performing Arts, opened in late 1989. The 150,000-square-foot structure, on the southwest corner of the campus, was made possible by a challenge grant from the Lied Foundation Trust.

The Heartland of America Park opened in 1990 on the riverfront in Omaha. The park's featured attraction is a 15-acre lake with a 305-foot lighted and computerized dancing fountain.

Peacocks that roam the grounds are a big attraction at the Henry Doorly Zoo.

The Lied Jungle (left) at Omaha's Henry
Doorly Zoo has 1.5 acres under the 80-foot-
high roof. Built with funds from the Lied
Foundation Trust of Las Vegas, the tropical
rain forest will feature jungle habitats from
Asia, Africa, South America, and Australia
and eventually will have about 3,000 species
of plants and 125 species of animals. Its
grand opening is planned in April 1992.

The Henry Doorly Zoo's vast collection of animals, birds, and fish includes the rare snow leopard.

Giraffes often offer a humorous touch at the Henry Doorly Zoo.

The ConAgra Frozen Foods Headquarters is one of four buildings on the new ConAgra campus at the east edge of the Old Market in downtown Omaha. The buildings include the ConAgra Corporate Headquarters.

The Old Market area of downtown Omaha has been one of the city's major tourist attractions for many years. In the first half of the century, the area was the home of open-air businesses that offered fresh fruits and vegetables. The Old Market shops, restaurants and boutiques cater to young and old and everyone in between.

The superhighway cloverleaf ramps are a help to drivers as they get on and off the thoroughfares, and they also are impressive from the air. Shown is the Interstate 680 cloverleaf at West Dodge Road in Omaha.

Ollie the Trolley is a familiar sight in downtown Omaha as it hauls passengers from the major office buildings and hotels to the Old Market area and back.

Omaha Chamber of Commerce

The Mutual of Omaha Dome, in front of the headquarters building on Dodge Street, offers an unusual view from below. The company, with assets of more than $7 billion and nearly eight million policyholders, is the second largest individual and family health insurance company in the nation. With more than 6,000 employees, it ranks as the largest private employer in Omaha.

The Omaha branch of the Federal Reserve Bank of Kansas City occupies nearly three square blocks in downtown Omaha. The bank moved to its new quarters in May 1986. It provides many services, but primary functions include providing currency and coins and check processing for financial institutions in Nebraska.

The birthsite of former President Gerald R. Ford, the nation's 38th chief executive, is located at 3302 Woolworth Avenue in Omaha. The birthsite was developed by Omaha businessman James Paxson. Ford was born Leslie King, Jr. His parents were divorced when he was two and he took the name of his step-father, Gerald R. Ford. The Fords moved to Grand Rapids, Michigan, when Gerald was an infant.

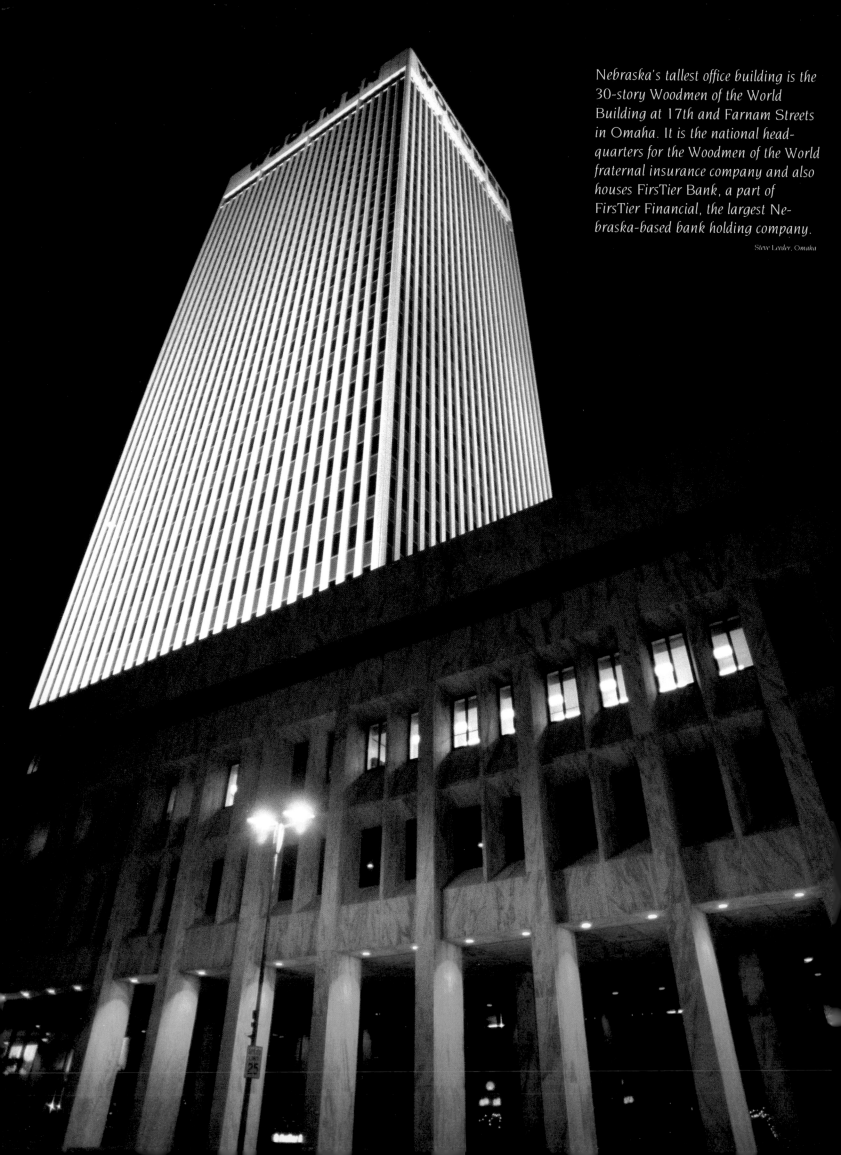

Nebraska's tallest office building is the 30-story Woodmen of the World Building at 17th and Farnam Streets in Omaha. It is the national head-quarters for the Woodmen of the World fraternal insurance company and also houses FirsTier Bank, a part of FirsTier Financial, the largest Ne-braska-based bank holding company.

Steve Leeder, Omaha

Omaha's Memorial Park at 60th and Dodge Streets
is eye-catching in winter as well as in summer.

The trademark statue of two orphan boys is the symbol of Boys Town on the west edge of Omaha. Boys Town is a non-profit, non-sectarian organization that has been the home for thousands of abused, abandoned, and neglected children over the last 75 years. The inscription on the statue reads: "He ain't heavy, Father . . . he's m' brother."

Boys Town is an incorporated Nebraska village with 75 homes on the 1,300-acre campus. Six to eight children live in each home with a family teacher couple. Boys Town has its own post office, police and fire departments, high school, middle school and vocational career center, and a working farm with 800 acres of arable land.

The Old Mill office park south of 110th Street and West Dodge Road is one of the newest and largest in the Omaha metropolitan area.

Peony Park (left) in Omaha is the state's oldest and largest amusement park, catering to fun lovers year-round. It offers dances in the pavilion during the winter and outdoor fun all summer.

Omaha Chamber of Commerce

The Union Pacific Museum, housed in the railroad company's headquarters building at Fourteenth and Dodge Streets in Omaha, offers a walk through railroading history.

With the fall of communism in Eastern Europe, the mission of the United States armed forces is changing. In June 1992, the Strategic Air Command will disappear and be replaced by the Strategic Command, or STRATCOM. It will marry the Navy and Air Force managers responsible for the smaller arsenal of strategic nuclear weapons. Offutt Air Force Base at Bellevue, which has served as headquarters for SAC since its inception following World War II, will become the headquarters for STRATCOM.

The Strategic Air Command Museum at Offutt Air Force Base traces the history of military aviation from the start of SAC in 1946. It has 31 aircraft on display, as well as an exhibit building that includes Space Age artifacts and a film explaining SAC's role in the defense of the United States.

Omaha's Central Park Mall at night is a sight to
behold. The mall offers an outdoors lunch experience for
hundreds of downtown office workers during the summer
months. Outdoor concerts are common attractions.

The Omaha Community Playhouse, in both physical size and membership, is the largest community theater in the nation. It attracts more than 125,000 theater goers a year to its main stage auditorium, which seats 600 people, and the newer 250-seat auditorium that offers flexible staging for many of the newer scripts. The Playhouse is home to the Nebraska Theater Caravan, its touring wing that has presented productions in 41 states and Canada.

Great Plains Black Museum

The Great Plains Black Museum at 2213 Lake Street in Omaha is housed in the original Nebraska Telephone Company building and offers artifacts and research material dating to the first blacks to come to the Midlands. It opened in 1976, the nation's bicentennial year.

Great Plains Black Museum

The Music Room at the Great Plains Black Museum traces the history of African-American music in America, from marching music to jazz.

The Omaha Airport Authority commissioned five major sculptures as part of its recent expansion program. The last and largest of the works is Dance of the Cranes *by John Raimondi of Boston, Massachusetts. It marks the entrance to Eppley Airfield and provides a symbol for the airport. With 15 tons of bronze measuring 60 feet high, it is the largest bronze sculpture in North America.*

The
Storz Fountain
Court at Joslyn Art
Museum provides the
setting for many of the museum's
programs and events. The Joslyn
schedules about six major special exhibitions
and a number of smaller presentations each
year. The temporary shows complement Joslyn's perma-
nent collections, the most noted of which is its collection of
art of the American West. Joslyn is the only art museum in the
nation to have a Center for Western Studies.

Omaha Symphony

The Omaha Symphony Orchestra, shown here with the Magic of Christmas Chorus, scheduled 54 performances in 14 series during the 1991–92 season. The orchestra with its Chamber Orchestra, SuperPops and Classical series, is directed by Bruce Hangen, musical director and conductor. The orchestra or its components travel 2,500 miles a year with performances in Nebraska, western Iowa and either South Dakota or Missouri. The orchestra is Nebraska's largest professional arts organization.

The Orpheum Theater, first opened in 1927, is the home of the performing arts in Omaha—the Symphony, Ballet Omaha, and Opera Omaha. After refurbishing, the 2,750-seat Orpheum held its second grand opening in 1975 and is busy almost every week with road shows or Omaha arts groups.

In 1990, Opera Omaha presented an Opera Adventure, which included nine performances of opera in the park for kids. About 6,000, mostly children, attended. The 1991–92 season schedule had 13 performances of three operas at the Orpheum Theater. The Ensemble of Opera Omaha presents in excess of 100 classroom workshops and performances annually to an estimated 36,000 children and adults throughout the state.

Nancy Rose and Reed Scott danced the starring roles in Ballet Omaha's production of Romeo & Juliet at the Orpheum Theater. Ballet Omaha presents four productions each season in Omaha and gives 35 touring performances in Nebraska, South Dakota, Iowa, Missouri and Kansas.

The reception room at the General Crook House at Fort Omaha is shown in its Christmas decor. The restored house, built in 1879 for Gen. George Crook, is operated by the Historical Society of Douglas County and is available for tours.

Christmas at Union Station is an annual tradition at the Western Heritage Museum in Omaha. The museum, located in the former Union Pacific depot, is noted for the Byron Reed coin collection and its vast historic photo library, along with several eras of walk-through history.

Roadway Confluence *is the name of the sculpture at a rest stop near Sidney on Interstate 80. The sculpture was done by Hans Van de Bovenkamp of Tillson, New York.*

Engineer Jim Reinders of Houston, Texas, a Panhandle native, built the Carhenge sculpture on his family's land north of Alliance in 1987. The controversial collection of 31 cars was buried in a fashion to resemble Stonehenge in England. Scientists have speculated that Stonehenge was an ancient religious center and astronomical observatory. Carhenge has attracted visitors from across the country.

Morrill Hall in the University of Nebraska State Museum on the UNL campus
also is known as Elephant Hall for its outstanding displays of fossils, biology, and
anthropology. Its collection features the world's largest fossil elephant. The museum
also boasts the Health Science Gallery, the popular Encounter Center and the
Ralph Mueller Planetarium, which presents the drama of the universe through sky
shows, laser entertainment and astronomical exhibits.

The Brownville Museum, now operated by the town of Brownville, is housed in the dry-docked Meriweather Lewis dredge that plied the Missouri River for the U.S. Army Corps of Engineers in the 1940s.

Pioneer Village

With more than 50,000 historical items displayed in 26 buildings on 20 acres, Pioneer Village in Minden is Nebraska's top privately owned tourist attraction. The buildings on the green include a country school, a blacksmith shop, a general store and more. It has attracted more than five million visitors and is open every day of the year.

Pioneer Village

A 1902 Cadillac is among the 350 antique cars on display at Pioneer Village. It also has 100 vintage tractors and the oldest known steam-powered merry-go-round, with rides still five cents.

The Stuhr Museum of the Prairie Pioneer in Grand Island in Hall County is one of the outstanding attractions in central Nebraska. It features the childhood home of the late Henry Fonda, one of America's best-known actors.

Lincoln Chamber of Commerce

Jim Denney, Omaha

The Sheldon Memorial Art Museum on the University of Nebraska, Lincoln campus was designed by Philip Johnson. It houses one of the finest collections of 20th-century American art, including paintings, sculptures, graphics, crafts, and photography.

When the state contracted to erect sculptures at 10 rest stops along Interstate 80 across Nebraska at a cost of $575,000, it caused quite a controversy. Only eight were ever built. It cost $100,000 in state tax money and the balance was paid for with funds from the National Endowment for the Arts and contributions from Nebraska businesses. One of the sculptures, near Ogallala, is Up/Over by Linda Howard of New York City.

155

The Robert Henri Museum in Cozad is named for the famed realist artist who lived his early years in the Dawson County community. Robert Henry Cozad was the son of John J. Cozad, the city's founder, whose family lived in the hotel that is now the museum from 1879 to 1883. The young Cozad changed his name to Robert Henri after attending school in the East.

Della Hendricks, Cozad

Nebraska's one-house Legislature is unique among America's state governments. Here, State Sen. Ernie Chambers of Omaha, one of 49 legislators, makes a point from the floor.

Omaha Chamber of Commerce

Described by architects as the nation's first truly vernacular state capitol, the Nebraska State Capitol (right) was constructed during the period from 1922 to 1932 at a cost of $1 million. It was built on a pay-as-you-go basis and was debt-free when it was completed. The Sower atop the golden dome has become a symbol of Nebraska.

James L. Fly, Li

The perfect ending for a perfect day could be a family walk at sunset at Holmes Lake in east Lincoln.

Lincoln's skyline at night is dominated by the State Capitol showered in lights.

Something for all ages in Lincoln is the Folsom Children's Zoo and Botanical Gardens. Animals such as this camel can be petted by the children in the "Critter Encounter Area" and a miniature train circles the zoo.

Topping off a fun-filled day at Hannibal Park in Beatrice, Bill and Brandi Hofeling take advantage of the water fountain.

Closing the generation gap, little Sarah Fettin faces off with her grandfather, Don Meisinger of Omaha.

Nebraska long has been noted for its beautifully constructed and maintained rest areas along Interstate 80. This one near the Seward/Milford interchange in Seward County is a perfect example.

Les Hosick, Stockville

A rare sighting in Nebraska is this one of a bobcat, photographed near Lime Creek in southern Frontier County. Bobcats are opportunistic predators and are found sparingly throughout the state where suitable habitat exists.

Mark Dietz, Bellevue

A baby raccoon caught in the photographer's flash gives a look of surprise. These nocturnal foragers are common throughout Nebraska.

The beautiful monarch butterfly also can be found in every part of the state. This pair was captured by the photographer at Neale Woods on the north edge of Omaha.

Mark Dietz, Bellevue

The prairie chicken is common in Nebraska's Sand Hills and has become one of the testiest game birds for hunters.

Mark Dietz, Bellevue

Todd R. Leif, Concordia, Kansas

Capturing the feeling of solitude are these horses in the sunset near Hastings in Adams County.

Almost scary is this foggy morning sight of a boat attached to a dock on a Cedar Creek lake in Cass County.

Robert Paskach, Omaha

Lee R. Mason, Alliance

Sunsets in western Nebraska can be spectacular, as this one near Alliance attests.

Just as the sandhill cranes are a sight to behold
when they take to the air by the thousands, this
aerial photo of the cranes roosting on the Platte
River near Kearney offers another perspective.
With more than 500,000 annually, Nebraska is
host to the largest concentration of cranes in the
world. It is the state's largest wildlife spectacle and
attracts thousands of tourists each year.

Nebraska Game and Parks Commission

The North Loup River inspires oohs and aahs as it winds its way through Blaine County five miles east of Brewster.

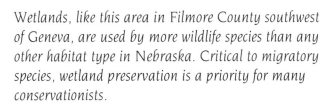

Wetlands, like this area in Filmore County southwest of Geneva, are used by more wildlife species than any other habitat type in Nebraska. Critical to migratory species, wetland preservation is a priority for many conservationists.

Kent Klima, Omaha

The intricacy of a spider's web takes on a beauty all its own.

Wildflowers sometimes can nearly swallow the countryside in the Sand Hills as is the case with these sunflowers and cleome.

Kira Gale, Omaha

Mary and Nancy Schaffert, Curtis

Beauty is where you find it, such as this arrowhead marsh at the upper end of Wellfleet Lake in Lincoln County.

A plant-clogged marsh in Bellevue's Fontenelle Forest offers an unusual photo opportunity.

Kent Klima, Omaha

Winter doesn't lessen the beauty at Fontenelle Forest in Bellevue.

Mark Dietz, Bellevue

Tim Vrtiska, Beatrice

Sunsets are special in the Midlands, but the
moon setting at sunrise can be just as beautiful.

The Nebraska Sand Hills have been cited as
being among the natural wonders of the world.

Nebraska Game and Parks Commission.

Jim Bahm, Norfolk

The Elkhorn River in the fall is a thing of beauty as it takes a 90-degree turn at the Yellow Banks Wildlife Area near Battle Creek. Nebraska's public hunting lands, like Yellow Banks, encompass some 750,000 acres on over 260 state and federal areas scattered across the state. This comprises about two percent of Nebraska's total land area, which means most hunting is done on private lands with permission from the landowner a must.

Ann Appelt, Ainsworth

Just One Bite *is the title given this photo as a tree seems about to devour a board.*

Garry Sader, Plattsmouth

Ripples on a Plattsmouth sand pit near Merritt Beach offer a tranquil setting for a woman and her cat during a fall stroll.

Fred Thomas, Omaha

*This view of the Niobrara River looking south-
west from more than 300 feet up is considered
one of the most beautiful sights in Nebraska.
The site is on land owned by the Nature Conser-
vancy in Keya Paha County south of Norden.*

"Reflect on the Past,

Celebrate the Present,

Prepare for the Future"

Computers will pave the way to the future for Nebraska and the nation in a high-tech world. Educational institutions are trying to keep pace with classes such as this AutoCAD (Computer Assisted Design) course at Omaha North High School.

Looking east from the Nebraska Educational Telecommunications Center, located on the Unversity of Nebraska-Lincoln's East Campus, is the satellite dish "garden" that gives the center the technical capability to offer Nebraskans an array of television, radio and telecommunications services.

The Santee plant of Becton-Dickinson and Company has several product lines assembled by its 21 employees, most of whom are members of the Santee Sioux tribe. Shown working at one of the assembly positions is Pauline Red Wing, since retired. Among other products, the plant assembles a diabetic take-home kit and an isofilter used in separation of fluids. The Santee plant, opened in 1975, operates as a part of the Becton-Dickinson plant in Columbus.

Helping to make Omaha among the world leaders in telemarketing is the Marriott Hotel Worldwide Reservation Center. The company, with about 1,000 employees, observed its 20th anniversary in Omaha in 1991. There are more than 10,000 people employed by 24 telemarketing firms in the city.

One of the largest manufacturing plants in Lincoln is the Kawasaki Motors Manufacturing Corporation, U.S.A., with about 500 employees in a 600,000-square-foot building that combines manufacturing, offices and warehouse space in northwest Lincoln.

Among the products manufactured at the Kawasaki Motors plant in Lincoln is the Jet Ski watercraft. The plant also produces motorcycles, all-terrain vehicles and utility vehicles, with about 100,000 units produced each year.

One of the newest office buildings in Omaha is the 1200 Landmark Center office complex built by Beta West, Inc., on the south side of the Central Park Mall. It is adjacent to the new U S WEST Communications data center.

Steve Leeder, Omaha

A planetarium at King Science Center is available to students throughout the Omaha Public School District as well as community groups. Another planetarium is located at Burke High School.

Marc V. May, Omaha Public Schools

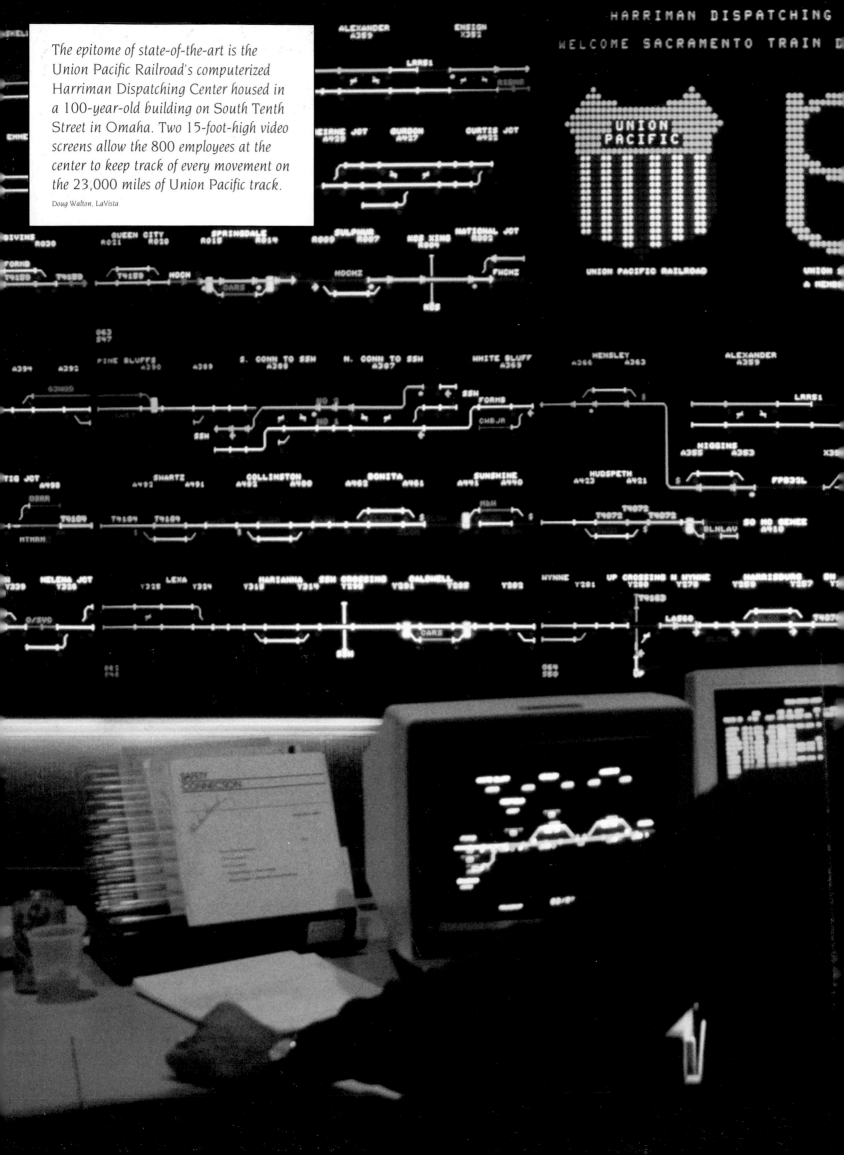

The epitome of state-of-the-art is the Union Pacific Railroad's computerized Harriman Dispatching Center housed in a 100-year-old building on South Tenth Street in Omaha. Two 15-foot-high video screens allow the 800 employees at the center to keep track of every movement on the 23,000 miles of Union Pacific track.

Doug Walton, LaVista

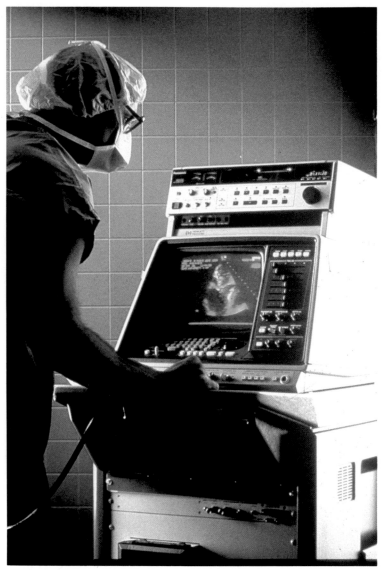

The echocardiography lab in Creighton University's cardiac center at St. Joseph's Hospital helps Omaha maintain its prominence as one of the top medical centers in the Midlands.

An Omaha Public Power District substation in northwest Omaha offers a view of the massive network required to feed electricity to the state's largest metropolitan area.

Duncan Aviation of Lincoln has grown over the last 35 years to become one of the largest privately owned business aircraft service companies in the world. Located in a 240,000-square-foot facility at the Lincoln Airport, Duncan Aviation has 575 employees. Shown is the maintenance and refurbishing of general aviation aircraft in progress.

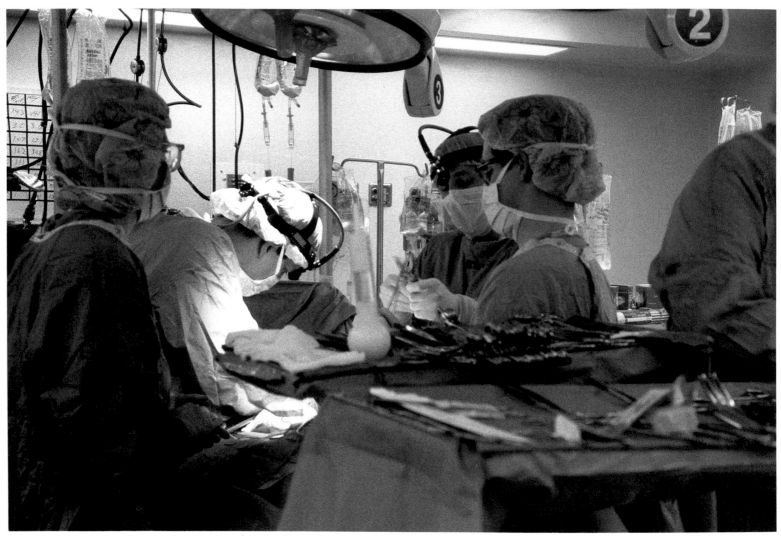

Under the direction of Dr. Byers W. Shaw, Jr., the University of Nebraska Medical Center in Omaha has become the second-largest liver transplant center in the country. Shown is Dr. Shaw's transplant team during the delicate surgery.

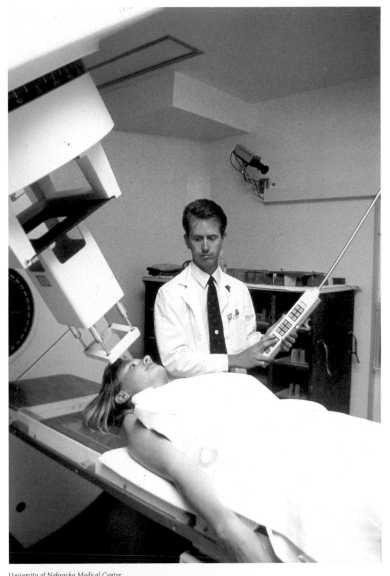

The linear accelerator, a radiation device used for cancer treatment, is operated here by David Granville, a radiation therapy technologist at the University of Nebraska Medical Center.

University of Nebraska Medical Center

Robert Campos, standing, owner and president of Campos Construction Company, the largest Hispanic-owned construction company in Nebraska, goes over a construction project with Gary Hopkins, an estimator for the firm. Started in 1977, the construction company has grown to 45 employees and contracts for jobs throughout the Midwest.

Jim Denney, Omaha

AT&T Network Systems, operating in the former Western Electric plant in southwest Omaha, is the largest industrial plant in Nebraska. It has 44 acres under roof on the 340-acre site and employs 3,200 people.

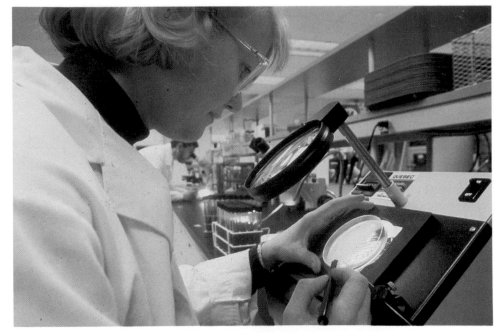

Microbiologist Diane West is shown in ConAgra's new Product Development Laboratory on the ConAgra campus east of the Old Market in downtown Omaha.

ConAgra

The Omaha Public Power District's nuclear power plant at Fort Calhoun can generate 492 megawatts of electricity. The district's nuclear plant and its other plants, coal-fired units at North Omaha and Nebraska City, combine to produce 1,867.2 megawatts. The OPPD plant is one of two nuclear plants in Nebraska.

Jim Denney, Omaha

Expressions of wonder are not unusual for the students taking a computer class at Druid Hill Math and Computer Center, an elementary magnet school in the Omaha School District. As Nebraska heads into the 21st century, the challenges of industry and society will be in the hands of today's children.